This book belongs to
a girl of strength and courage
whose very special heart always
knows what to do:

_____

(your name here)

You are forever great
and truly incredible.

Also by Ashley Rice

For an Incredible Kid
You Are a Girl Who Totally Rocks
You Go, Girl... Keep Dreaming

Library of Congress Control Number: 2009903157
ISBN: 978-1-59842-350-1

BLUE MOUNTAIN PRESS is registered in U.S. Patent and Trademark Office.

Certain trademarks are used under license.

Printed in China.
First Printing: 2009

Blue Mountain Arts, Inc.
P.O. Box 4549, Boulder, Colorado 80306

GIRL POWER

Penelope J. Miller's
Guide to Being
Great

Ashley Rice

Blue Mountain Press™

Boulder, Colorado

☆ An Introduction
by Penelope J. Miller

My name is Penelope J. Miller, and I am the narrator of this book. I want to start off first by saying "hi" and letting you know that a girl in the world like you has the power to be anything she wants to be!

In these pages you'll find lots of stuff to inspire you as you make your way in the world. I'll share with you all the secrets of girl power, as well as my own thoughts and advice on how to be the greatest "YOU" you can be!

What is girl power exactly? Good question. It's hard to define exactly — but it includes things like real spirit, determination, and courage. Girl power is knowing deep down inside that you can succeed. It's never giving up. Girl power is standing up for what you believe in... for yourself and for other girls, too.

Girl power can be found in lots of places. It's in the future you want to create. It's in the true support of good friends. Girl power can help you be more creative, incredibly smart, and very strong in every part of your life — but first you have to believe in it!

Remember: with girl power in your heart, you can change the world!

Your true friend,
Penelope J.

You have the POWER within
yourself to make good
decisions. You have the
beauty within yourself to
live a wonderful life. You
have the courage within
yourself to face any challenge.
You have the strength within
yourself to make a difference...

You have the uniqueness within
yourself to be extraordinary.

You've Got
What It Takes

Sure it feels great when
everything's going right...
then there are some days
we've got to face situations
that don't seem as bright.
If that ever happens to you,
don't worry about it:
try not to get down or feel blue.
You see, you've got what it takes
in your brave and true mind
to overcome any mountain —
no matter how steep,
no matter how high.

Just focus on "Right now" –
not the future or the past...
just this one moment,
Right here, where you stand.
Then do your very best
to understand what you've <u>got</u>:
the wonderful power
of your own heart, soul, and hands...
which is much, much more than a lot.

The more **challenges** that you **face**...
the more **Races** that you **Run**...
the more **hills** that you **climb**
to the **top** and **overcome**...
the **stronger** grows your **heart**,
the **wiser** becomes your **soul**.

Each **time** you **travel**
down a **bumpy** or unknown **road**...
the **swifter** become your **feet**:
with **every** hard-won,
honest **victory** —
and yes, **even** with each **defeat**.

Penelope on What It Takes to Be Great

Some people just accept what is handed to them in life — be it very much or very little — and fashion a world out of that.

Other people make their way through the passing days determined to grow up and one day give something back...

Whether they know it
or not, these people often open up doors
for others, ask questions, and change
lives and minds, too... for they believe in
bright stars in everything they do. They're
tough and kind and amazing and true. And
they never give up.

That's you.

How to
Stay
Strong

Take some time every day
to Remember the things
that make you happy...
Whether it's the flowers
outside your door or the wind
Rushing through the trees...
a moment or a smile
or the last time you spent
a really long time laughing.
Hold these things close
in your heart...

They'll keep you strong.

Believe in Yourself

Believe in the way you are
and the way you will be.
Believe in the things you say.
If you should ever doubt yourself
in any way,
don't think twice about it.
Don't worry too long
about whether you'll find a place
for yourself in the world —
you belong.

You'll get where
you're going someday.
For no matter what happens,
you will find a way.
Believe in the way you are
and the way you will be.
You are a shining star
in this world.

A girl in the world
can do most anything
she puts her mind to.
She can WRite a book.
She can start a band.
She can become a doctor.
She can dream and plan.
She can handle adversity.
She can stand up tall.
And in all these things,
she is beautiful.
She is strong.
A girl in the world
is a wonderful thing.
She can do most anything
she puts her mind to.

Never forget you've got
the chance to dance.
Never forget you've got
the chance to fly.
Never forget that you're
your own "I"

with possibilities in every
new and old thing.
Never forget that every
day's a dream…

that you've got
the chance to sing,
to live, and to touch the sky.

Never forget to let
your heart fly...
or that the world itself
can be magic.

How to Find Your Butterfly Wings

Step 1: Close your eyes

Step 2: Imagine a set of wings

Step 3: Think about your dreams

Step 4: Listen with your heart

Step 5: Count from one to ten

Step 6: Believe your wings can fly

Here's your pair of butterfly wings.
They'll help you do many great things.
You've always had the ability to
"fly" to your dreams.
And in your heart...
now all you've got to do is leap.

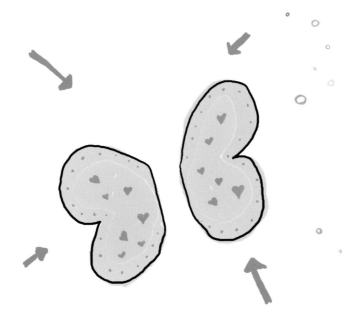

Stand up for what you know
    is Right.
Always Remain brave and strong.
Keep the fight in your heart —
whether the place where you are
is beautiful... or not quite so.

Everywhere you go,
hold on to what you believe.
You might also inspire others to do the same.
This is one of the most important things
that you can do...
for you and for others like you
that you meet along the way.

A Few Words from Penelope

I want to tell you that you are talented and ambitious. I want to tell you that you are wise beyond your years.

I want to say that you are skilled and have an instinct for what you do.

I want to say that you are brave, true, and sincere.

I want to tell you to keep your spirit and love for life — and that you will go far.

I want to tell you that you're better than just good...

You're great!

There's Power In...

individuality hope

truth

determination

friendship intelligence

heart strength

willpower

creativity

Keep your girl power growing.

Believe in your dReams.
Believe in who you aRe.
Make choices with your bRain.
Make decisions with your heaRt.
Define a finish line.
Finish what you start.
Make fRiends and
make everything you do
woRth doing.

A Powerful Girl like You
can Make Amazing
Contributions to Her
Community and Beyond

The possibilities
are endless...
You could be an
astronaut, a scientist,
a mathematician,
an activist, an actress,
a doctor, an athlete,
an artist...

What will you do?

Poem for an Amazing Girl ("Did I?")

Did I make a difference
for having been here?
Did I help someone through
a difficult situation
or touch that person's heart?
Did I make someone think
or laugh or grin?

Was I a good teammate,
acquaintance, or friend?
Did I remember friends' birthdays
and honestly care?
Did I stand on my own two feet?
Did I live each moment –
even the hard parts –
with all my heart?

You are an amazing girl
who does these kinds of things
every day.

You're like a Daisy...

A daisy is a very
special flower that needs
sunlight,
dreams,
and goals
to grow
up strong...
and your dreams
are growing
by the hour.

You've got
flower power!

You Have a Guardian Angel

Guardian angels are everywhere –
looking out for each of us all the time.
If it ever seems like your angel can't be
found, that's just because there's a way for
you right around the bend, at the end of a
"Rainbow" or at a new fork in the road –
but you yourself have to find it. When you
really need her, your guardian angel will be
right there: in the faces of your friends,
your family, or your pets; in the letters or
postcards you send or you get... And if you
believe in them, you'll soon see that there
are in fact guardian angels everywhere...
including one for you, too.

When in Doubt, Read This Out Loud:

I won't be any less than my best.

I won't stress over
small things when
I know that tomorrow
they can't hurt me.

And I'll keep pressing on
to see everything
I know I will see...

Because I believe in my life
and I believe in tomorrow...
in my heart and in my dreams.

ReMembeR...

Nothing can compaRe
to youR spiRit,
youR style,
youR smile,
youR laughteR.

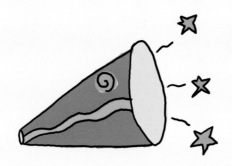

Penelope's Keys
to Girl Power

Dance and laugh hard
and grin a lot
in your heart.
Follow your dreams
(it's always worth it).
Don't ever stop smiling.
Don't ever stop trying.
Stay on your toes.
Reach out as far as
you can reach
and then reach farther.
Don't forget to
rock the world.
And — oh yeah:
shine on.

The Power Is Yours

You've got strength and courage...
lots of things to see and do.
You've got plans and dreams,
and you know how to see things through.
You've got books to read,
places to be, and people to know.

You've got the power
inside yourself
to do many great things!

Your spirit, individuality,
and determination
will lead you to your dreams.

Always use your imagination,
your heart,
your love for life,
and your gift
for persevering...
and your life will be
extraordinary (it already is).

You Have the Power Within You To...

🌸 Try new things

🌸 Make a success story of your life

🌸 Overcome obstacles with perseverance, intelligence, dignity, and a sense of fun

❀ Discover new paths

❀ Make your life your own

❀ Blaze a trail toward all
you can be

❀ Follow your dreams

❀ Be anything you want
to be

There may be times along the way when you feel alone. But you never really are! There are always friends to be made and new adventures to discover. There are friends and family members who respect you for who you are...

Wherever you go...
you are loved.

The Power of Friendship

Once in a while, you find
someone who makes you smile...
someone who makes you grin...
someone who makes you laugh
until you're rolling
on the floor with laughter –
tears coming out of the
corners of your eyes –
until you can't remember
why you were stressed
or sad about something...

And you're just happy
to be there in that moment,
laughing and smiling
with someone who
knows you so well.

That's the power
of friendship!

The PoweR of SpiRit

YouR spiRit is like youR heaRt –
when you Reach up oR out,
it helps you fly.
YouR spiRit can be youR love
foR diffeRent people oR things –
it'll lift you way up
if you fall sometimes.
YouR spiRit says:
"Don't eveR give up,"
"I'm in youR coRneR,"
and "Let's go!"

It cheers for your hopes
and the dreams of other hearts
who pass by.
Your spirit can pull you
through anything.
It will keep you strong.

Each day you can start
   again.
You are free to make
   your way in this world.
You are free to lose.
You are free to win.
You are free to let loose
   in this world
and to laugh as much as
   you want.
You are free to face
each day as if it were
the first day of your life.

Powerful girls
work to make their
goals and dreams
come true.

Write down the names of powerful girls you know or have heard about:

1. _____
   (your name here)

2. _____

3. _____

4. _____

5. _____

6. _____

You have the ability to
change the world.
Stand up. Stand tall. Speak up.
Always try your hardest.
Trust yourself.
Try to look at the long term.
Whatever you are doing,
if you love it,
keep on trying.

Don't worry about yesterday...
just be here now.
Don't worry about the future
or what it might bring.
Don't worry about the past —
what did or did not happen.
Be here now
where you are needed...
where anything
can happen.

A star
for all you do...

A star because
you're bright...

A star to watch over
your days and dreams
each and every night...

A star because
you're unique...

A star because
you're kind...

A star because
you're you:
keep on shining bright!

Penelope's Wishes for You

I hope each day
is better than the one before.
I hope your face
hurts because your smile
is so big.
I hope your days
are filled with sunshine
and laughter.
When you wish,
I hope you wish big.